spongers

RIOT STORIES

DRAWINGS: GILL THOMPSON

ACKNOWLEDGEMENTS

Thanks are due to the estate of the late Sonia Brownell Orwell and Martin Secker and Warburg Ltd. for permission to include a passage from *The Road To Wigan Pier* by George Orwell. Also to .... for permission to use the poem *England* by A.S.J. Tessimond from *Voices In A Giant City*.

To everyone who offered encouragement.

Printed in Great Britain by
Redwood Burn Ltd., Trowbridge, Wiltshire, and
bound by Pegasus Bookbinding, Melksham, Wiltshire.

ENGLAND

The ancient custom of deception;
A Press that seldom stoops to lies —
Merely suppresses truth and twists it,
Blandly corrupt and slyly wise.

The Common Man; his mask of laughter;
His back-chat while the roof falls in;
Minorities' long losing battles
Fought that the sons of sons may win.

The politician's inward snigger
(Big business on the private phone);
The knack of sitting snug on fences;
The double face of flesh and stone...

The 'incorruptible policeman'
Gaoling the whore whose bribe's run out,
Guarding the rich against the poor man,
Guarding the Settled Gods from doubt...

The smile of privilege exultant;
Smile at the 'bloody Red' defeated;
Smile at the striker starved and broken;
Smile at the 'dirty nigger' cheated...

England of rebels — Blake and Shelley;
England where freedom's sometimes won,
Where Jew and Negro needn't fear yet
Lynch-law and pogrom, whip and gun...

England of clever fool, mad genuis,
Timorous lion and arrogant sheep,
Half-hearted snob and shamefaced bully,
Of hands that wake and eyes that sleep...
England the snail that's shod with lightning...
Shall we laugh or shall we weep?

A.S.J. Tessimond. Autumn 1938.

When I first saw unemployed men at close quarters, the thing that horrified and amazed me was to find that many of them were *ashamed* of being unemployed. I was very ignorant... The middle classes were still talking about 'lazy idle loafers on the dole' and naturally these opinions percolated to the working class themselves. I remember the shock of astonishment it gave me... to find that a fair proportion of these beings whom I had been taught to regard as cynical parasites, were decent young miners and cotton-workers... They had been brought up to work, and behold! it seemed as if they were never going to have the chance of working again. In their circumstances it was inevitable, at first, that they should be haunted by a feeling of personal degradation.

George Orwell. 1937

AND WHAT HAS CHANGED?

INTRODUCTION

"You get treated like dirt... I keep looking for a job and all the time you're thought of as some kind of *sponger*... It's almost as if it's a crime to live."

UNEMPLOYMENT in Great Britain is now higher than at any time since the Thirties, and rising more sharply than in any other major developed country. As I write the number of people without work is nearing four million — almost half are under 25 years old.

Many have never had a chance to work and the way the situation appears at present they never will. It is a cruel irony to have been born at a time of unparalleled prosperity and optimism when the future now holds only uncertainty and distress. Their age and lack of privilege continue to prevent young people taking any hand in improving matters (the opposite of course being de rigueur for success in the political system).

Sheer frustration has already helped to fuel destructive riots. I don't condone this action but it is hypocritical of our society to blame the youth when those in power offer no solution, not even recognition and understanding of the problem.

No real attempt has been made by the government to look into the social problems which unemployment causes — the terrible and increasing strains on once-strong communities, families, individuals. (And do the trades unions care? Do the employed themselves constitute a defensive vested interest? How many so-called Socialists are to be trusted?) Those who haven't experienced the dole may say "Why all the fuss, it's not so terrible, no-one starves anymore". But the feelings and struggle are still the same, only from within — the attack on the human spirit. To start treating the jobless as people, instead of as merely statistics, would be a start.

During last years election campaign all Ministers avoided making any forecast about future job prospects except in vague and general terms (talking all day, saying nothing). And only by artificial schemes and administrative tricks has Mr. Tebbit been able to reduce the unemployment total — i.e. by merely falsyfying the figures. This must end.

There are ways which could succeed. The future does not lie with leisure services — superburgers and space invaders — as our leader believes (Oh my God. Brilliant etc). Britain, like every other industrialised country, does not lack work to be done. For example housing is in chronic shortage and by 1985 will be in crisis. Our cities are decaying. The same is true of hospitals, schools and community centres, while the infrastructure of roads, rail, transport and power supply, that is essential for a thriving industry, is long overdue for improvement. Putting these deficiencies to right isn't making work it is instead using work, work that needs to be done, to create and preserve real and lasting jobs, especially in the neglected unemployment blackspots. And (for all you cynics) if this scheme was carried out with determination it would probably pay for itself sooner rather than later. This is merely one idea — there are literally thousands of possibilities.

'Spongers' is not just another anthology. It is not a 'clever idea' around which to build a collection of poems, but, I hope a way to convey the thoughts, feelings and observations of young people on the dole. (I know). However it is not an endless moan about unemployment. Far from it. There is anger and despair (of course) at seeing hopes and dreams vanish, but also glimpses of love and strength. And this is hopeful because there will be no change until together we begin to speak out against this situation and use our voice and energy more fully to force honest action. Starting now. **Dave Potter**

TERRITORY

A web of cracks catch a gap in the pane,
selfish iron sheets cover the beckoning frame,
inside are rooms that could be called home
but group 4 make sure they're left alone.
The doors have been nailed up.

Meanwhile, round the corner, with rooms to spare,
the man in his house makes sure he takes care
to ram home the bolt at twelve o'clock,
closing the heart as he turns the lock,
tight as the seal on his mortgage.

While across the park the scroungers settle down
and in her parent's home a lonely girl is crying.

Chas

DON'T JUST SIT THERE

When you've been stabbed so many times,
When you've slapped your heart on the butcher's table,
And watched the bastards slice and steal it as souvenirs,
When you've forgotten yourself
And wonder whether the sun is shining behind the curtains:
Open them for God's sake.

Nicola Connelly

SEARCHING

*I feel angry when I think of all
the beauty that was bestowed upon
me the day I was born.
I feel angry because, over the years,
I accepted only the ugliness in growing up
to affect my self-development — the beauty
inside of me gradually took a back seat
as I searched each day for:*

*something to do
a reason for living*

*As each day passed I continued my search
for a meaning to life; I became
frustrated as my search proved futile
but still I looked — outwardly — for a reason.
I found nothing except reasons to be ugly.
Then, by accident, I looked inwardly
and found the answer to my search.
I am here to live happily and freely.
Sharing my love with everyone I meet.
If I can do that — which I know I can.
I will become a free spirit — which I know I am.*

Jim Creelman

(A QUESTION OF) PRIORITIES

We had a by-election at our home town this week
Me school were on the telly and we had cameramen down our street.
Me dad said he'd not vote, that it were "all a waste of time",
But me mam can be very persuasive;
"You'll vote Labour or else", she cried.

I could not understand the fuss, no reason would satisfy me
why our diet was party manifesto for breakfast, dinner and tea.
Me mam said it were significant, that she'd explain when I grew up
But to me it weren't half as significant
As when Liverpool won the cup.

And so we made the papers, our town were front-page news
More important than Ken and Dierdre (Not quite as Andy and Koo)
Yet now it is all over, only hope can fill the void
'tho me mam's dead chuffed that Labour won
And me dad's still unemployed.

Delbec

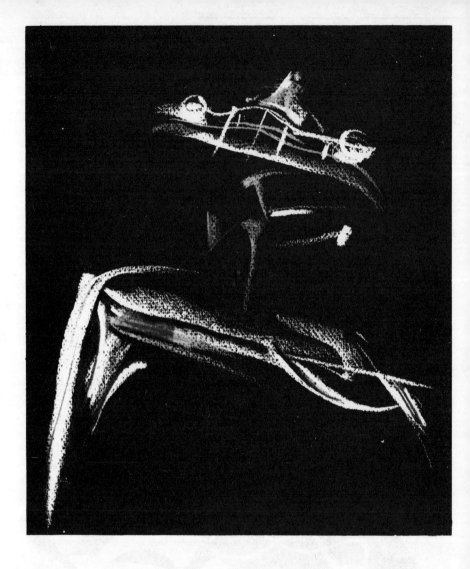

CAN'T AFFORD LUXURIES ANYMORE

Dear Diary

I asked my daddy if he would buy me an ice-cream today
but he said he couldn't afford it
and when I asked him why
he said it was because he's lost his job
and that he didn't have the money to spare
for luxuries anymore

I didn't know ice-creams were called luxuries
Well anyway, I spent all my time looking for it
in the garden
in the park
but I couldn't find his job anywhere
I even asked my best friend's dad
but he just laughed
and said he was looking for one himself
I wonder why he laughed
I wouldn't laugh if I had a job
and then lost it
I'd be very sad
My other friend Darren
he's older than me
he said I should go to the job centre
because that's where they find jobs for people
but when I did
a man pointed to a queue of people
and said they were all looking as well
I can't understand that
because you'd think with all these people looking
that someone would have found it by now
But anyway
the man did give me a note
and told me to tell my dad
to call in
and he would see what he could do for him
So I gave daddy the note
and he promised he would call in
first thing in the morning
but later I overheard him say to mummy
that lots of people who've lost their jobs
have been to the job centre
Well I hope dad's wrong
and that the man does find his job for him
because he is making mum very unhappy
with all his shouting
and it's not mummy's fault
he lost his job
he should be more careful with things

But I'm even more upset
because while dady hasn't got a job
I can't have luxuries anymore.

John Walsh

"HA! HAPPY CHRISTMAS"

Families enjoy themselves,
kids open their presents,
the house is warm
with the feeling of merriment.

The old lady sits there,
one bar on the electric fire,
wrapped in a blanket
breathing slowly.

Her breath can be seen
it reaches the ceiling
and then disappears
like her hopes for joy.

She thinks of the better times,
but the memories, she can't recall,
they have faded,
blended with the wallpaper.

She struggles to get up
strain shows on her face.
Years of helping others
but who wants to know now?

Gradually she admits defeat,
her mind and heart
agree also.
She sits there, silent and cold,
Like the snow.

Alex Dickinson

A NIGHT ON THE TOWN

The city was built for poets,
A parade of constant events.
The neon whistles in colour,
And Nelson's earning his rent.
But yet, but yet,
Some miss the social safety net.

Down In The Underground

A woman who wouldn't have worried
If the escalator has never moved.
And an unknown human in a coat of thread,
Just showing the world a scum of hair,
Unchanged from arrival to departure.

Later Outside

A man topples over
Broken by the clear-eyed dawn.
Losers
Don't owe the world a thing.
A clever thought to scribble down
On my homeward train.

Tony Dixon

Like a caricature of themselves
The complacent nibble and chatter.
...Another death in Ethiopia.
"Dullish day dear"
...Another two thousand redundant.
Conversation over cocktails.
"Five pounds. Well it's the least I could do."
Ulterior motives make me sick.
Omniscience fades the scene to elsewhere.
"I love you"
..."Is Mike in?"
Buckles and buttons cease to be useful.
..."Is Chris in?"
His hand higher
Acting pleasure is self-convincing.
Love? Ulterior motives make me sick.
The cloth of his suit triggers bored aggression.
Muscles flex under a Perry like a blow-up Tarzan.
A fist helps cover the Telegraph in blood
...City life?
Impressive applause of vomit on Vogue
...City style?
Reverse class discrimination.
This is a cry from the heart,
Be HONEST to yourself!

Giles Fraser

BITTER TRUTHS

Kids sheltering in shop doorways
Confused, hating
Their expectations shattered —
As per usual.
It's so cold and industrial,
A 'slit your wrists' picture,
Just like our lives —
Disintegrating.

Bob Graham

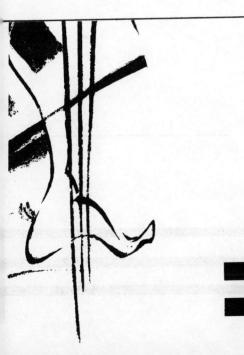

MICK

As he lay helpless
There was nothing any of us could do
But sit and wait
Until the hour
When Mick would be no more.

Still in his youth
He never knew love
Or triumphs
Or even life.

His ambitions were plentiful
But Mick wasn't to know
That they could never be fulfilled.

Home comforts were far away
When each function failed,
Hospital smells lingered
Not that Mick knew any different.

No one cried
When he died
But silence hung in the air.
We all knew that lying there
Could easily have been one of us.

Jane Griffiths

COMING HOME

Back to single beds.

Not grin, but grimace
As the taxi pulls up
And she falls out.
Met by dad.
I help her luggage
Reach the door.
He doesn't move,
And we stare
Into the distance,
Through each others heads.
Talking is not to be the answer.
Taxi clock whirs, money melts
And I run back.

The faces continue to stare,
One smiling and waving, one not.

Steve Grimmond

SULLEN STREET

Woolies, Burtons and superdrug
beckoning lights to capture the money spending bug
loud ringing tills
solicitors bills
a cut price defeat
runs the length of Sullen Street.

Records, books and cards
betting shops and Wimpy bars
burning sun and melting tar
as carbon monoxide pours from endless cars
bidding a hasty retreat
rushes the crowd in Sullen Street.

Memorial plaques
generation gaps
Oxfam and help the aged
news stands portray horror front pages
glooms always so concrete
enclosed inside Sullen Street.

Stand and talk
speechless and walk
people and shops
forever pulling down blinds
solitude designed with a constant closed sign
with barriers and divisions
searching providence but musing indecisions
the pacing of lives in downtrodden feet
the sadness in eyes that glazingly meet
pains now so indiscreet
installed inside each Sullen Street.

Viv Wheeler

THE USUAL

In my day everybody worked, no question
(Now there's unemployment, remember?)
When I was young the sun shone
(It still does)
We used to have a good time; work hard, play hard
(Not enough money, not enough smiles)
I feel sorry for you
(But pity won't do me any good)
But why can't you be normal?
(So what's normal?)
Why can't you be like me?
(I'm myself, nobody else)
How do you know you won't like it if you don't try it?
(I know what I hate, trust me)
I admire you for it, of course
(Pity **and** admiration? I can't believe that)
But what if. . .
(I could go on supplementary)
And what would you do. . .
(I'd still be looking)
I don't like to see you down like this
So what do you expect?

Rosemary White

In shock of death
Acquaintances sickeningly multiply.
Their reminiscences rarely
Strike a feeling chord.

Involvement seems more important
Than the painful WHY?
Cries of "He wasn't like that"
Grasping for a piece of the Gore-light.

I am no better —
A false sorow
Crossing my pained face.
Partly relishing the
Involvement with death.

Until now. His sister looked grave.
I shied away, scared
To broach a tender subject.
Her hair, and heart, hung limp.

Her tale was factual,
The method sensitive.
— He ran crying, unfollowed
— Folding his clothes and jumping naked.

Comprehension often comes
More easily when told
What did happen
By a shocked participant.

Her casualness belies
Her inner tears/tears.
— The body hasn't been found
— But give it six weeks.

The real pain oozes from here.
The agony speaks quietly,
Numbed, even stilled.
A silent scream.

Steve Grimmond

LOVE ON THE DOLE

"He'll never get a job" — they say
so maybe I should marry a millionaire
and spend my days in sunny climes
draped in finery, eating delicacies
— the world is my oyster, laid at my feet.
But you buy me chips when I'm hungry
and at nights in the pub a half pint of beer
and I love the way you look at me sometimes,
turning all my dreams into realities
— besides, I've never met a millionaire.

Cathy Harris

RENE

rene walks where people
where angels fear to tread
but it's because she hasn't got her glasses on

oceans part for rene
who doesn't notice this
because she doesn't think anyone notices her

rene phones me up sometimes
when her boyfriend has gone out
she thinks that the units won't register
if she talks in a whisper

Helena Hinn

TIMES LIKE THIS

Times like this
I wonder about my own
Ignorance,
I question what right
I have to complain.
I see kids with no legs
Smiling
And men with shot faces saying
They're doing their best.
My own depression
Makes me ashamed,
Old excuses sound
Pitiful.
See these starving babies,
Plagued by flies,
And realise
Justice is a farce —
Part
Of that Utopian thing.

Life is still a priceless
Privilege.

Mark Hockton

THE PUNCHLINE

Have you heard the one about
The desert filled with green love?
Well it wasn't funny anyway
Blared the sirens in lavender home
Where the tragic comedians jump
Over fires of shaving cream
In a hell-hole worth living for.
See the comedians roll
Up their sleeves and slaver
Over junk,
Cut arteries and pose for photos
In front of starving African children
Who simply love Hollywood.

And I've forgotten the other names
Of people who died younger than me
Who told the same old jokes
About life's dark corners
You know. About poppies
Once a year. Macho etcetera
And a bouquet of funny men
In vests and silk pyjamas
And Eskimos drink Coke
Indians die, and I ask
You for a penny's thought
In a year of pseudonyms
And strange faces. Win friends
Fly to far off places, buy a gun
Live in empty swimming pools
And dream nightmares for Jesu's sake.
I hope you have a nice time in England
Fill it with green love and laugh.

Graham Hopwood.

ROBBIE

The inconsiderate sun heralded a new day, waking Robbie as it did so, who
                                                          was not pleased.
Robbie was twenty, into double figures, it was all downhill till thirty now.
At least that's what his brother had said and Kevin knew everything.
So many things to do, thought Robbie, so many options.
A walk down to the job centre perhaps to pick one of the many jobs on
the board, there were always so many he didn't know which one to take.
Kevin said the jobs were cosmetic and that the cards were just filling
in cracks that were on the verge of becoming large holes — he says some
wierd things does Kevin.
Robbie leaned over and picked up the blowpipe from the floor, a present
on his eighth birthday and still a regular around the bedroom.
Carefully he aimed at the small ornaments on the wardrobe and fired.
The china swan exploded into tiny pieces and Robbie smiled.
A knock on the door interrupted Robbie's contemplation.
"Robbie. It's nearly three o'clock, are you getting up today or not?"
It was his mother, who thought he should get up and go and look for a job.
She didn't realise there weren't any — she watched too much telly, so
Kevin said.
Robbie came to an important decision around 3.56pm.
He would get up for tea.

John MacGregor

RECESSION PRAYER

Our Lord, who art in number ten,
Hallowed be thy name.
May thy ministers come and do thy will,
But not in the backstreets as in the suburbs.
We'll pay you this day our daily taxes,
And forgive you your trespasses,
As long as we've got bombs for those who trespass against us.
And lead not the masses into prosperity,
But keep them from employment.
For thine is the industry,
The power and the wealth,
For ever and ever; Amen.

Gary Williams

THE PEOPLE SHOP
A wet day
Water on the glass door
Push it open
A blast of boiled air
Inside so quiet
Is it a library?
Or a church?
No — it's the people shop
People for sale
Buyers on the cards
Old people, new people
One with orange hair
All shuffling, looking
Without hope
With nothing but a battered kind of pride

Rosemary White

SUMS

> half a days military spending = amount needed to eradicate malaria
> 1 jet fighter = money for 40,000 village pharmacies
> 1 tank = 40 classrooms
>
> Q.E.D.

John MacGregor

TURN LEFT AT TESCO'S, AND CARRY ON DOWN TO CAMBODIA

Personalised tea-cups
A trip to the store
Anonymous rate demands on the thirteenth floor

Crumpled snapshots
A letter incomplete
A T.V. detector van crawls around our streets

A well-thumbed novel
A pint and a laugh
Our leaders pay homage to the Cenotaph

The T.V. Times
The dog to feed
Our schools have no books for our children to read

A kiss for a sister
Money lent to a friend
A voting slip placed in an unconcerned hand

Too few doctors
Illness and disease
Do they sell black shirts at Sainsbury's?

L. Middleton

NEWLY WEDDED WIVES

Young wives reading '19' at 23
Sit in a stew smelling of Boots own
Await in pent up agony
Their hero, late again
His dinner's dried up
And I'm feeling rough
I've washed the nappies
I've fed the cat
The bugger's in bed
So that's that
Gets out her knitting
And designs for living
Dreams of old boyfriends
Married, or dead, or both
Wishes for excitement
Dreams of Anthony Andrews
Sucking her breasts
Gets a shiver...
Feels like a young wife
Alone, depressed and agonised
Stuck with a house, a hubby
And a blissful bond of love.

Mark Davies Markham

REACHING

A crisp, cool midnight,
Under the eve of Spring:

The stars are out tonight —
Or are they satellites?
Above our heads
A crystal bowl
Beneath our feet
The broken glass

(1/3/83)   H.H. Neilson

JOB HUNTING

He shook me warmly with his cold hand.

(In keeping — I had mis-read —
his door did not say Personal Manager).

He sat me down, by command.

"The onus is on you."

"Why this?"

"Why that?"

Not a flicker of emotion until he said
"I have to ask you these questions."

As I left I congratulated him.

A fake compassion for his lack of success?

I had outwitted him by equal lack.

Colin Nixon

TOWN LIFE

You live in a town
a town everyone loves
with its pubs, discos, a standard of living
supermarkets — pre-packed —
relaxation through pills that cure all ills
to stagnate in this sluggish pond...
and people who differ are fools to you now
you've forgotten a life (long ago)
you were different then people still say
though it's been over ten years now
and the memories have been buried deep...
for now you're a part of the town —

the town everyone loves.

Glyn Pearl

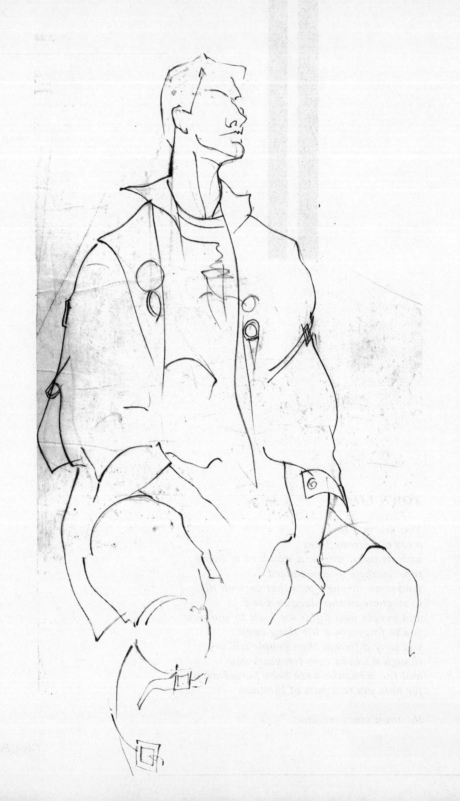

SOCIAL SUPPLEMENT STUFF

He couldn't fill in the forms. You see
They'd taught him moonies and dodging maths
They'd never tried to tell him how, instead
They'd taught him to be a Maes 'G'* lad.

It wasn't so bad, "no school or nothin'".
They said it wasn't bad (at first).

I met him in The Harp, had a pint and
"She's a nice girl," he said. Didn't know
She wasn't alone in her clothes now, thought
It only took six months anyway.

"Nice girls still don't," they said, but
"Come back to my flat."

He gave his brother all the forms to fill
"Sixteen quid for two weeks sick" (been done)
"Fuckin' M.I.C. aye, better off on the dole."
In the pool room I watched the video, far away through fag smoke.

"They offered me my job back", he said.
"No chance."

(Another fine). They caught him this time
Pissing up a wall in the dark
Down by the football club. He'd
Been eating curry — I can taste him now.

"He didn't have nothin'," they said.
I think I agreed.
"My brother's O.D.'d," another he said.
"Oh aye."
"Maes 'G'," he said. "Maes fucking 'G'."
And that was all.

Karon Wright

*Maes 'G' — Large council estate. Also known as 'The End of the World'.

MAN AT THE TOP

Scurry along
The early morning
Blur — Terylene and
Plastic.

Sell yourself
Again and again
To buy
Happiness — read twisted security.

Not a care in the world
(For others)
An attractive veneer to life
(Which cracks).

You say I'm wrong?
Why can't you look into my eyes?

Dave Potter

GIVEN UP

Jug bellied
gut jellied
skin slung
wind wrung faces,
pouched like slugs on a rim.
Slouched in smokey rows
of slack-strung clothes,
they've sunk, gratefully, to a cess.
Shrunk before the blast of battle.

They've long since accepted
their odour, a stink
that clings and is
clung to. These streets
are streets they've always
tramped. Now they're stamped like fauna in grey pages.
Either that or bottled
or canned or frozen.
Processed through a method of madness.

These unfortunates are, in some way,
limbless.
I mean crippled of
the lust, the reaching. . .
No teaching can restore that.
They've given up.
Gone from the fighting
to the fearing
and the merciless rain of days.

Paul Simmonds

We are — the bank blank generation,
No fat sugar-daddies
To keep our poverty sweet.

We once — had hope — confidence,
No longer true,
Mind murdered in the prime of life.

We are — the press pressed generation,
"Do you sniff glue sonny"?
Answer politely — in disillusioned tones.

We are — the lonely flat-trapped,
Tolerable poverty — until
Our black and white friends flicker out at midnight —

Closedown time!

John Warburton

THE PAY DAY CORNER

The pay day corner of the street
Where nobody stands still
And money is paper thin
On homeless walls.
A congregation of lovers tell secrets
To newspapers buying the evening edition of fun —
Tomorrow will come with a bang and a black eye
I'll sell you my thoughts in return for their peace of mind.

John Watkins

THE APPLICANT

Must be smart numerate and literate
and clean their teeth three times each day
must be between 21 and 40
and wear size 8 shoes
must be able to deal with people
and hold a 25 yards egg and spoon race certificate
must be adaptable and work weekends
must know how to say Sir and Thank You
must have experience of this kind of work
must know their place and provide excellent references
must have a shining spotless record
or eyebrows will be raised in resolute resignation
must must must must must must must must must must must

Andrew Smith

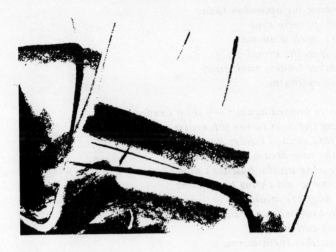

LOVE STORY

(inspired by recent talks to check immigrant marriages. Jan '83).

We will watch them secretly
see how often they touch
how often they touch (it must be at least once a day)
if they remember anniversaries and birthdays
if they look happy all the time
we'll look into the history of each case
and if they claim it's love at first sight
we'll send a man round to look into their eyes.
It's really just a matter of discretion.

Andrew Smith.

Went out looking for optimism today
Most of the shops were shut
But they don't stock it anyway
So I lost myself in the crowd
Watching market traders pack away
Everyone else's optimism

Schoolkids noses pressed against toy shop windows
Soul boy trying the door to the job centre
Housewives from council estates peering through
Windows in the new dream show houses
The old girl eyeing up the butcher's dog
Wished someone would throw her a bone
She'd have a dogs life anyday
Some come to town when the shops are open
Call themselves earlybirds
Everyone else wishes them worms
(It's all optimism in a way)

Down the high street everyone's mouth seems to be open
No words, just open mouths
Maybe someones tied their vocal chords in a knot
Maybe they're looking for optimism
Bet if they found it they'd swallow it whole
And clamp their mouths shut
Never speak to a soul
So that no-one could talk it out of them

Walked home by the canal
Passed the scrapyard — rust
Passed the tanning factory — stench
Passed the weaving sheds — silence
All the way fish floating dead with their
Mouths open
Like dead souls painted on black skies
With their mouths open
Waiting for the kiss of life
Looking for optimism

And people keep telling me it won't last forever
But you've really got to work at it to keep your
Dreams together
And
so
tomorrow
I'll
take
it
down
to
the
benefits
office

And
smile
all
the
way
through
her
telling
me
to
Fuck
Off!

Sheila Tierney

SUBWAY

The iron bars stop the bikes from riding through,
Graffitti on the once whitewashed walls,
Glass from the vandal-proof lights on the floor
And the ever acrid stench of fluid and filth.
I walked down the slope,
Leant on the bars, felt sick,
Bitter acid taste in my mouth,
I crouched in the corner,
Couldn't be sick.
And old lady walked past —
Looked disapprovingly.
The putrid feeling wouldn't go.
Three blokes walked from the shadows,
They stared at me, I couldn't think.
The pain in my stomach twisted,
I stood straight, began to walk away.
They smiled — menacincly.
I walked to the bus-stop, leant against it,
They smiled and stared,
The first kick landed, doubled me up.
I was sick on the pavement,
The bus came.

Nick Triplow

BAN THE BLAME

The cover plan books a table for two
In the aftermath of circumstances
Too alien to surmise or be grateful for.
A wind shadow blows apart from the seemingless shore
Waving to a drowning soul too weak to cry.

A boat passes the corpse several days later
And hoists a flag so others may take note.
It wasn't the water that killed the body flesh
But the deep hatred that existed between
Two struggling forces bent
On possible revenge.

John Watkins

A MESSAGE FOR THE FUTURE

People live for today
People live for tomorrow
But he lives in the past
His thoughts and hopes of years gone by
Just drifting away
Hopes that have faded to dreams
He feels rejected, cheated and unwanted
Sitting confined in his lonely room
Scared and frightened
Too afraid to leave the security of his dreams
Is this justified? Is this human? No!
To begin to make peace and unity grow we must
Cease to cheat one another
We must wise up
We never were wanted, none of us
Our future must lie together if to survive is
Our goal
We must unite to create the solid bond
Between our hearts.